D0538590

HOW TO LOOK AFTER
YOUR
HUMAN

First published in the USA in 2016 by Frances Lincoln Children's Books,
74-77 White Lion Street, London N1 9PF, UK
QuartoKnows.com
Visit our blogs at QuartoKnows.com

Text copyright © Kim Sears 2016
Illustrations copyright © Helen Hancocks 2016

ISBN 978-1-84780-787-8

Illustrated in gouache

Edited by Katie Cotton
Designed by Nicola Price

Printed in China

9 8 7 6 5 4 3 2 1

HOW TO LOOK AFTER YOUR HUMAN

🐾 A DOG'S GUIDE 🐾

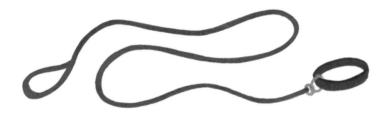

BY MAGGIE MAYHEM

with help from
KIM SEARS

illustrated by
HELEN HANCOCKS

Frances Lincoln
Children's Books

• Contents •

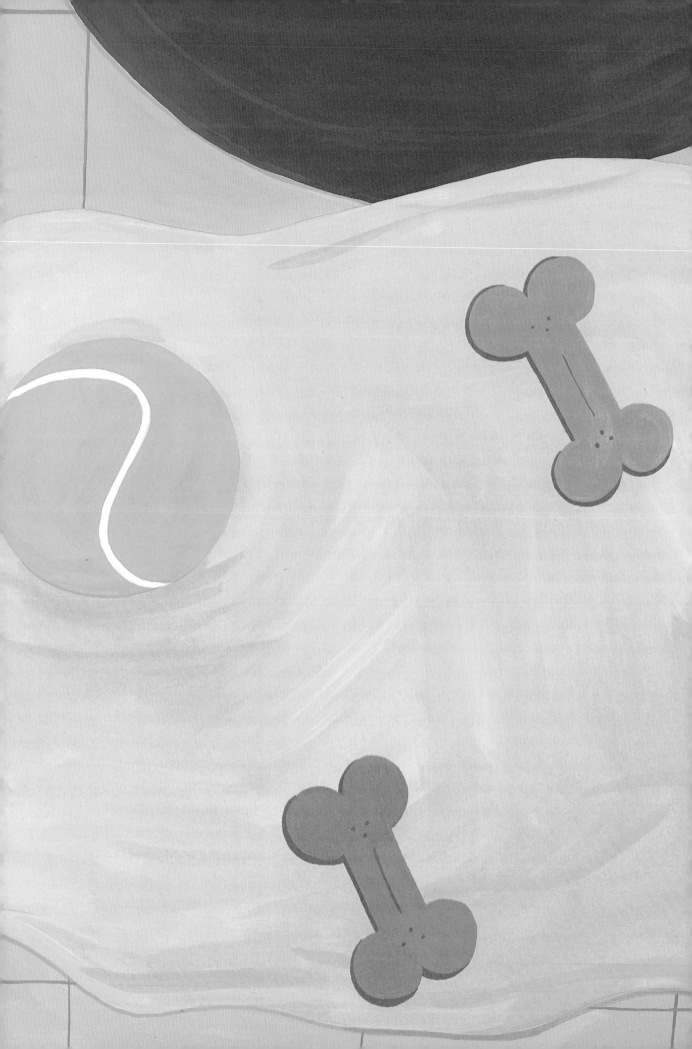

Dear Readers,

Keeping Homo sapiens is an immensely rewarding practice, yet one that requires a firm paw and hours of patience. As a keen human enthusiast, with years of knowledge developed over endless walks and cuddles, I believe that I'm well placed to educate you all in what makes this relationship so unique.

My goal over the next few pages is to guide fellow canines in how to get the most out of their non-furry friends: from diet to discipline, socialization to sleeping arrangements. I write from one wagging tail to another, yet hope that humans themselves (should they be able to read) may find this basic guide illuminating and helpful.

With fondest bottom sniffs and wet kisses,

MAGGiE

Moi

First though, a bit about me. My name is Maggie and I am an eight-year-old Border Terrier. I live just outside London with my brother, Rusty, and we own two adorable humans, plus an assortment of their extended family and friends.

Someone somewhere once said that great things come in small packages, and as a member of the terrier family I am inclined to agree with them. I'm obviously biased, but I feel that there is no better way to see the world than from twelve inches off the ground. Everything looks bigger, for a start, especially the important things such as biscuits, pillows, and rainbows. Obviously this means that scary things are larger too, but that's fine because as a terrier I'm genetically programmed not to be scared of anything.[i] In fact, while we're talking science, did you know that the terrier has a brain twice as large as a human?[ii] I'm not quite sure where I learned this from, but it's definitely true, and would explain why we are able to train Man to be such a biddable and docile companion.

But back to me. Though I may be a celebrity in certain circles, I'm not what would be described as a conventional beauty (think red setter, King Charles cavalier), nor am I of the exhibitionist persuasion (toy poodle, miniature poodle, standard poodle).

[i] Yet to be officially verified.
[ii] Also yet to be officially verified.

Here's a self portrait, which I've helpfully annotated for you:

My **coat**, as you will see, is a rustic muddy brown with the texture of steel wool. But before you get any ideas about this meaning Border Terriers are common little dogs that don't like cuddles, I'll have you know I love having my belly scratched as much as any of my fluffier friends. Just don't call me a lap dog.

I have velvety smooth **ears** that look like upside-down pieces of Toblerone. All dogs have exceptional hearing, but terriers like me are unique in that we have the exceptional ability to not hear things we don't like, such as instructions.

Border terriers have thick black **claws**, which are especially good for digging holes and tunnels. I like to help out in the garden and I'm extremely good at uprooting geraniums.

My **nose** gives me an incredibly strong sense of smell. I have a particular speciality in sniffing out small animals to chase.

CHAPTER ONE

HOW TO CHOOSE
YOUR HUMAN

HUMANS: A BASIC INTRODUCTION

Humans and dogs have shared each other's lives and homes for thousands of years, and each partnership has the potential to be of the most rewarding and fulfilling variety. It is important that you fully understand that each human is different, and the choice of whom you spend your life with will have implications on the direction your time together will take.

I have compiled a brief list of easily identifiable dog-friendly people. This is by no means comprehensive and, indeed, humans are complex creatures— it is impossible to categorize and label them so simply. Yet I hope the following may help you make an informed decision when it comes to choosing your human(s).

THE FAMILY

Possibly the most common humans you will encounter. Homo sapiens are sociable creatures that like company, and as a result enjoy spending time with high numbers of their own kind, as well as other species (hence the reason that they make suitable companions for dogs in the first place). The family traditionally combines large numbers (two or more) of humans spanning both genders and multiple generations.

The positives to this are endless: expect a busy, bustling home filled with warmth and laughter. Frequent family meals ensure that you are guaranteed regular table scraps. The higher the number of humans in your household, the higher the cuddle ratio. Often, a large, "family-style" car is included in the package which means frequent trips en masse to exciting places like the beach and the park.

· Important Note ·

AVOID the family if you are not of a sociable disposition, are averse to lots of noise, and struggle to tolerate small humans under the 4-foot variety. A word of warning: as previously mentioned, a family of humans will frequently come with extra members of different species: cats, fish, horses, gerbils, or even reptiles. If you are not prepared to share your home with any of the above then the family is not for you, and you must look elsewhere.

iNDiViDUAL HUMANS

Living with just one human has huge advantages, undivided attention possibly being the most significant. The range of available single humans is vast and covers the entire spectrum of mankind. I've subdivided this section in order to help you identify a few notable characters.

· Important Note ·

NEVER assume that your lone human will remain so forever. You always need to be prepared for the possibility that he or she will one day invite others into your home. If you cannot get your head around this idea, then owning humans is not for you.

The Dresser-upper

This breed possesses a frightening array of canine couture for any occasion. From yellow raincoats for drizzly days, to inflated pumpkin bodices at Halloween and elf suits at Christmas, no outfit is too adorable or ironic. Perfect if you're into that kind of thing, but if you'd rather be seen in the coat you were born with instead of a faux-fur-lined aviator one during the winter, avoid.

The Feeder

....

This type of human enjoys spending time in the kitchen and
will most probably slave away for hours whipping up unique
and interesting dog treats. Highly likely that instead of being
dished out meat straight from a can, you will be fed lovingly
cooked meals served to you piping hot on a bone china plate.
However, any mutterings of moving you toward a gluten-free
or vegetarian diet should be firmly ignored.

The Aspiring Athlete

Avoid at all costs if you are allergic to large quantities of high-intensity exercise. Will try and convince you to become a "running buddy," will want to play endless ball games (not always a bad thing), will leave large quantities of sweaty Lycra lying around the home (good if you are into playing with smelly socks).
Note: protein shakes don't agree with the canine digestive system and you should refrain from stealing these.

The Amateur Photographer

This breed will take a lot of pictures of you. When you're sleeping, when you're eating, when you're playing, and when you're just sitting. Will most likely encourage you to perch on historical landmarks in order to capture your bemused expression. Frequently speaks in weird tongues ("bokeh," anyone?). Does not find the smear of a wet nose across their 50mm-lens funny OR endearing. Good if you've a large ego, but patience and the ability to give good face are key.

CHAPTER TWO
COMMUNICATION

COMMUNICATION

Once you have chosen your human, you will no doubt want to know what they are saying, both verbally and physically. This can be daunting at first, but the following guide should help to demystify their behavior for you.

BODY LANGUAGE

Smile

The human tail wag. Identified by the corners of the mouth turning upward; often revealing teeth. A smile occurs when a human is happy, which is why humans owned by dogs are more smiley than others.

Laughter

An extension of the smile, but accompanied with unusual animal noises (snorting like a pig/squawking like a bird). Indicates that your human is very happy and has found something amusing. Don't worry, though, they are never laughing *at* you.

Frown

A smile, but upside down (no teeth . . . that would be terrifying). A frown expresses sadness, or worry, or even fear. All of the above can quickly be remedied by jumping on your human and physically licking the frown off their face.

Crying

Normally a sorrowful expression of sadness or discontent (although it can occasionally be a sign of extreme joy). It is often distressing to see your human in such a state, but remember that human tears contain healing powers, so you should try and get as close to them as possible. They taste salty, like the ocean.

Yawn

A lengthy opening of the mouth, often accompanied by a rough groan and/or elaborate arm stretching, meaning your human is tired and in need of sleep. All you need to know is that this is your signal to ask for food/to be let out for a pee/to go on long, vigorous walkies (delete as appropriate).

Waving

An energetic greeting or farewell, often employed from a distance. Although, confusingly, the same gesture is used to try to shoo a fly or mosquito.

HMM ...hmm

Scratching head

While this behavior can suggest confusion, inspiration, or vulnerability, most importantly it can be a sign that your human has fleas. If so, you should take action immediately.

ERM... ...ERR...

Twiddling thumbs

Nearly always signifies boredom. This can escalate to destructive levels swiftly so you must intervene and provide a distraction; I suggest throwing yourself onto the carpet and rolling your eyes madly, while trying to sing "Unchained Melody." This usually shocks them out of their behavior and they are unlikely to do it again.

Licking their lips

Usually a sign that your human is thinking about food. Point them toward the refrigerator.

Wrinkling their nose

Normally, this means your human has caught a whiff of a smell that they find extremely unpleasant. However, if this is done in your direction, it is obviously a sign that they would like an Eskimo kiss. Indulge them for a moment.

VERBAL LANGUAGE

Trying to understand the verbal language of humans is a total minefield. They produce thousands of different noises ("words"), altering the order, pitch, tone, and volume every time.

BLAH BLAH BLAH BLAH BLAH BLAH BLAH BLAH BLAH BLAH BLAH BLAH BLAH BLAH BLAH BLAH BLAH

If you are a border collie, there's a huge possibility that you enjoy devoting hours to the study of human language, and chances are you are fluent already. If you are another breed, however, I would suggest you come to terms with the fact that most of the time humans are talking nonsense anyway, and the following words are the only ones that matter...

Breakfast, lunch, dinner, cookie

All different words meaning essentially the same thing: food.

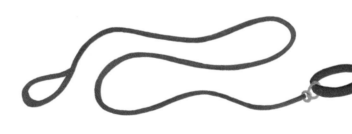

Walkies

We are leaving the house! Huge cause for excitement, unless it's raining.

No

I've never quite understood what my humans mean when they say this, but as they say it to me so often I believe it must be a term of encouragement. I suggest that when your human says "no" to you, you continue with the activity you were in the middle of, but with extra enthusiasm, to show them you've heard them and you appreciate their feedback.

FETCH!

??

Fetch!

As I touched on earlier, this is a favorite word of the lazy human. It is the word they use when they want you to pick something up for them. If you are a labrador or any other kind of retriever, you may enjoy this sort of activity. For the rest of us, however, I suggest adopting a look of disgust and simply walking away.

SiT!

Sit!

Humans will often ask us to sit down. I believe that they are simply jealous of our four legs versus their two, and they ask us to sit so they feel we are on even standing. It's nice to occasionally make them happy, and to show them we're willing to compromise. Don't ever agree to sit down on a stone floor though, unless you want a very cold behind.

COME !

Come!

This simply means that your human wants you to go to them. They may ask this when you are on the other side of the room, but they may also bellow this when you are many fields away, in hot pursuit of a rabbit. For both scenarios I give you the same advice: the choice is entirely up to you.

· Handy Tip ·

Conversation between you and your human is obviously going to be impossible—you don't speak the same language, after all. But if you would like to make your human feel as if you understand them when they babble at you indecipherably, simply stare at them intently and tilt your head from side to side. This usually satisfies them that they have made their point effectively, and they promptly allow you to return to whichever activity you were getting on with.

A note on bonding

Humans are ultimately a tactile, affectionate species, and their pack mentality means that they enjoy physical company. This is one of the reasons that we dogs so enjoy sharing our homes with them. It's important to show how much you love your human on a regular basis. Don't underestimate the importance of a tail wag or a wet kiss on the hand in cementing the bond between the two of you.

CHAPTER THREE

TRAINING

TRAINING

You should now have a basic understanding of the differences between the way dogs and humans communicate. Effectively letting your human know what you want from them takes lots of practice, but as they are malleable, semi-intelligent creatures, you should begin to see results quite quickly, and it will become clear that interspecies communication isn't all that tricky. As we progress to specific areas of training, bear in mind these easy steps to make sure that you get what you want out of your relationship with your human:

1. We should use positive reinforcement at all times. Humans don't respond well to scolding or telling off, so we should try to simply encourage and reward good behavior, and ignore the bad.

2. You should approach training sessions in a lighthearted, engaging manner; if your human enjoys herself she is more likely to benefit and be willing to learn.

3. Be sure to adopt the "little and often" approach. Your human will only have a short attention span so it's best not to bore them.

4. Make sure you end on a good note and then take a break to do something fun together, before revisiting what you've covered later on.

HOUSEHOLD MATTERS

One of the first things you will want to train your human to do is to clean up after you. This is not out of pure laziness but, instead, practicality—they have opposable thumbs so can carry out housekeeping duties so much easier than us. Begin with the most basic of exercises:

On the first day in your new home, choose a spot that is impossible to miss in a room that is frequently used, and go to the toilet.

I know, this goes against everything your mother taught you, but remember, you're doing this for the benefit of your human.

It's a bonus (though not essential) if you can find a cream-colored carpet—this shows up anything and will make a perfect blank canvas for your handiwork.

If your human is a bit slow to catch on, make sure you sit perfectly still, staring at the mess until they've dug out the rubber gloves and detergent.

You shouldn't have to repeat this exercise too many times before your human understands their cleaning role, and then you can start going to the toilet in the flowerbeds once more.

. Remember .

You shouldn't restrict this cleaning-up exercise to toilet training, however. In those tender, early days of your relationship, it's important to make as much mess as possible so that your human knows exactly what's expected of them. My brother Rusty learned to open the door of the refrigerator at an early age, and to test our humans' abilities with a kitchen floor strewn with vegetables, egg shells, and melted ice-cream. Once, he stole a jar of peanut butter and intricately smeared it into a shag pile rug, but I must make it clear that that is a rather advanced level of housekeeping and you shouldn't expect your human to willingly adapt to such demands. Ours just happen to be exceptionally well-trained in that department.

TERRITORY

Another area that needs to be addressed early on is that of territory—your human needs to be firmly educated about which area of the house is theirs, and which isn't. If you don't tackle this issue, before you know, it your human will be waltzing around as if they own the place!

The most important thing to get right is sleeping arrangements. If you can't provide your human with their own room then you will have to let them sleep in your bed (I've heard cases of humans taking the sofa and the dog the only bed, but quite frankly that's a bit primitive).

HOWEVER

You must never let your human forget that the bed is yours and they are merely a guest. You should always get tucked in first, making sure you're comfortable. I personally like to scrabble deep underneath the duvet, because the dark warmth helps me dream I'm chasing rabbits through their muddy burrows.

Whether you like to sleep high atop a pile of plump pillows or sprawl across the middle of the mattress like a starfish, your human will need to slot in wherever there's space. Once they have learned that, you can apply the same rules to any piece of furniture in the house.

POSITIVE REINFORCEMENT

As your relationship develops, there will, of course, be more lessons that you wish to teach your human. Whatever the exercise, you will need to reinforce good behavior and ignore the bad.

For example, my human once correctly identified that my whining at the biscuit cupboard meant that I would like a treat, so he got up from the sofa immediately to get me one. I showed him how good he'd been by wagging my tail enthusiastically and giving his cheek a big, wet lick.

HOWEVER

My other human once naughtily assumed that as I was muddy I would like a bath, so she began filling the kitchen sink with warm water and bubbles. I immediately ran upstairs and lay underneath my bed where she couldn't find me, to show her that I wasn't justifying such terrible behavior with a response.

CHAPTER FOUR

NUTRITION

NUTRITION

The average human will usually eat three meals a day, supplemented by a range of snacks where necessary. I know this seems a bit excessive, but you must remember that they have large bodies to feed.

Also, once you've read this chapter, I think you'll realize that having so much food in the house actually works out in our favor. But before I go any further, remember the golden rule when it comes to eating in your home: all food is to be shared. As soon as your human understands this, you've unlocked the key to both peaceful coexistence and permanently full bellies.

· Handy Tip ·

A quick word on dog food: you might not think it looks particularly appetizing compared to human food, but what if I told you a very clever dog intended it to be that way? Humans find our food revolting, so we get to eat an entire, uninterrupted meal that is full of all the nutrients and vitamins we need to keep being fabulous. Then we get to share our human's food too. Genius!

· Important Note ·

When supervising your human's mealtime, it's essential that you have one eye on what you want them to eat, and the other on what you want to eat yourself. Any successful relationship is about compromise, and knowing that you can pick up where your human left off is the key to good ownership.

HUMAN MEALS

Breakfast

is the first meal of the day, and it is traditionally announced in my household by a ritual face-licking from me while my brother Rusty sings a joyful accompaniment from the foot of the bed. Bacon, eggs, and sausages are all highly recommended (there is never a better start to the day than the scent of frying bacon filling the nostrils). I wouldn't bother with cereal and toast. Leave those to your human.

Lunch

is taken around midday, but often this can be underwhelming; humans often like to eat soups and salads that are quite boring for dogs. Sandwiches though, can often be filled with all sorts of yummy things like cheese, ham, or tuna (my personal favorite). Make sure your human shares bits of these with you, but don't be fooled into just having the crusts without any of the good stuff!

Dinner

is my favorite meal of the day, as it's usually the biggest and most exciting. You can expect a large plate laden with all kinds of delights, and by this time in the day your human will have eaten quite a lot so you can expect them to share a large part of their meal with you.

Sharing is caring

A polite human will offer to share food with you at the appropriate moment during their meal. As a species they are intensely food-driven, so don't be surprised if initially they are reluctant to part with morsels of their dinner. Perseverance here is key, and lots of gentle reminders should do the trick.

Vigilance

When your human assumes his place at the dinner table, your first job is to position yourself in direct line of sight. You should watch every single piece of food travel into their mouth so that you can be sure to catch anything that drops onto the floor.

Eyes on the prize

Those of you belonging to a larger breed may like to rest your head on their placemat at this time. As I'm small and can't reach the top of the table even standing on my back legs, I like to sit on the floor and simply stare, unblinking (humans appear to understand this subliminal messaging easily).

BARK!

If all else fails

A long trail of drool onto the clean floor is often a good idea, just to show them you mean business. If your human is of a stubborn disposition, then a slow, quiet whine as they are raising fork to mouth is often effective, but should be used as a last resort: if your eye game is good enough you shouldn't need to stoop to such measures.

Playing by the rules

From a well-trained human you should expect the rule of thirds: after two mouthfuls you should be given the third, and so on. Make sure you swallow without chewing to give yourself enough time to be ready for the next bite.

· Remember ·

You both need to pull your weight in order to coexist happily, so dogs should always offer to clean the dishes. I personally really enjoy this part of mealtime and have been known to spend a good twenty minutes licking the plates after a Sunday roast.

There are some delicious human foods that we should insist on sharing:

Apple

Not only are apples delicious and crunchy but they also freshen your breath. Let the human dispose of the core, mind.

Carrot

Carrots also clean teeth and freshen breath. Don't eat too many though, or they will turn your poop orange!

Yogurt

Super delicious and filled with healthy bacteria. Make sure your human invests in a variety that has a container large enough for you to fit your snout all the way in.

Hot drinks

I'm partial to a slurp or two of tea (milk, no sugar). However, you have to be incredibly careful—my brother Rusty was far too enthusiastic once and burned his tongue on a hot cuppa. He had to lick a marble floor for an hour in order to cool it down.

EXERCiSE & SOCiALiZATiON

I want to talk to you about "walkies." It is important for dogs and humans to get out and about in order to stay healthy and burn off excess energy. We are all guilty of becoming lazy in the comfort of our own homes, but the daily ritual of taking exercise forces us to meet new people and have new experiences.

· However ·

Don't let your human think they're calling the shots. Before you know it you'll be hooked up to a bungee cord and setting off on a 15-mile mini-marathon across the Appalachian Trail. I like to go on a walk for two reasons: to chase things (I am a terrier after all), and to make new friends. It is important to work out the kind of walk that is right for you, and then think about how your human can benefit. I may be stereotyping, but the following pages contain a few examples of different breeds of dog and the kind of walk they may be inclined to take.

Working dogs

If you are a spaniel or pointer, you may love walks in the forest where there are hundreds of birds for you to sniff out and flush from the bushes. But don't let your human get lazy while you run around having all the fun. When you take off after a pheasant, encourage them to follow. Running through narrow woodland paths and ducking under branches is great for their fitness and agility.

Pastoral dogs

Collies and other pastoral dogs love having a job to do, so really enjoy walks where they are constantly getting a squeaky tennis ball to chase through the grass. Keep dropping the tennis ball right at your human's feet: this ensures they keep throwing it for you, and improves their strength and concentration.

Natural-born swimmers

If you are a retriever or Newfoundland (both of whom have webbed feet), you might literally jump at any chance to get wet, be it hurling yourself in a blissfully cool lake, or simply soaking your belly in a muddy puddle. For some reason, humans never seem as keen as us to take the plunge while out on walks. This doesn't mean they can't feel involved though. Show them how much fun you're having by standing right next to them when you shake your coat dry after hauling yourself out of the water. Don't make them too wet though, or you'll have to put up with the smell of Soggy Human for the rest of the day, and trust me—it's not pleasant.

Terriers

Terriers like Rusty and I love walks where we can
chase things, be it a fluffy rabbit, mischievous squirrel,
or our other dog friends who love a good game of
tag. Be sure to make as much noise as possible so
that your human knows where you are most of the
time. A loud yap is also the perfect way of letting
everyone know what a good time you're having.

It goes without saying that if—on any walk—you have to be on the lead, make
sure your human is always behind you. This is to make sure they don't get lost
or get any false ideas of who's in charge.

Whichever walk you choose, do not neglect the training of your human. Remember that humans come in all different shapes, types, and sizes (as do dogs). Each individual is different and will have varying degrees of fitness. Some humans would happily run for hours across rolling hillsides, while others are content with a short stroll to their nearest coffee shop and back.

· Handy Tip ·

If you feel like your human could do with a helping hand in getting in peak condition, then take a leaf out of my book and take off after a field of sheep—I guarantee you will have never seen your human move faster, and they will end up red in the face and puffing harder than a steam train. Alternatively, follow in the footsteps of my good friend Buddy the springer spaniel, who likes to weight-train his human by pulling on the lead like a cart horse.

MAKING FRIENDS

Aside from ensuring that your human is physically fit, walks are a fantastic way for them to learn to behave sociably. We usually meet lots of other dogs on our walks and I'm sure you're the same; you'll have your regular buddies that you enjoy catching up with, and then you'll meet new dogs on occasion too. My best friends are a black Labrador called Willow (she runs really fast and lets me chase her for hours on end) and a cockapoo called Murphy.

We all have a crazy run around together and then we'll lie in the long grass nibbling at each other's coats and having a good old catch-up. And importantly, whilst I'm catching up with my friends, my humans get to spend time with their humans too, enjoying stimulating conversation and practising their communication skills.

· Be Prepared ·

Humans have the most unusual way of greeting one another. Instead of sniffing each other's bottoms they actually shake hands. I know, it sounds incredibly vulgar but we mustn't judge what we don't understand. I am merely pointing this out so that you don't stare crudely when you first see this happen (as I did).

Fun and Frolics

On a final note, walkies are good for mental exercise too. Try playing one of my favorite games: hide-and-seek. It will test your human's logic and problem-solving skills and strengthen the bond between the two of you.

It's incredibly easy for you to play, and can be done almost anywhere. Just choose a moment when you're off the lead and your human has their back turned—either chatting to another human, looking at their cell phone or (if you're really fast like me) blinking. Turn tail and run as fast as possible to the nearest cover. You don't want to go too far and get lost, but you want to make sure your human cannot see you. I know of a blonde labradoodle who once stood silently among a field of sheep for ten minutes before her human discovered her.

GROOMING & HYGIENE

Dogs and humans have drastically differing tastes when it comes to grooming and personal hygiene. Starting with the basics, you will need to be prepared to regularly wash your human. Those sensitive noses of ours will detect the most subtle change in body odor and so regular sanitization is as much for our own comfort as it is for their hygiene. I am of the opinion that if you want something done well you need to do it yourself, and this applies to cleaning humans.

Facing the issue

I like to give regular baths with my tongue at rolling intervals throughout the day. The best way of administering these baths is to pin your human onto a sofa or other large piece of furniture, with a paw on each shoulder, and start from the top of their head. The face seems to collect a lot of grime throughout the day, so you will need to spend a good deal of time on that area.

Spotting an opportunity

Alternatively, if I spot a human wearing shorts or a skirt, I do like to give their legs a quick clean—this is especially rewarding if they have just been doing exercise of some kind as you'll find their skin delightfully salty.

Bathtime
. . . .

When your human becomes so incredibly stinky that you can't bear to clean them yourself, it is best that you guide them toward the bathroom and run a nice hot bath for them. Never leave them unattended, mind you, because you never can be sure whether they've cleaned behind their ears or not.

When your human is in the bath, you should prop yourself on the edge and stare at them the entire time. A gentle growl works wonders if they've missed a bit.

It can be tedious work though, so if you're in need of a little refreshment, you can take a quick drink from the toilet bowl without letting them out of your sight.

Humans have insanely bad breath. I put this down to the fact that every morning and evening they have a curious habit of scrubbing their teeth with a small, bristly brush. Try to destroy these brushes at any opportunity—simply whisk one off to your favorite hiding place and chew it to pieces.

HAIR

Now while pretty much all dogs, whether they are male or female, are covered in hair (except the Chinese Crested, of course), most humans have more hair on their heads and faces than the rest of their bodies.

Some humans have long hair on the top of their head that takes a lot of washing, brushing, and drying. I've tried my best to brush it with my claws in the past but I've learned that they prefer to take care of this themselves—some of them get quite sensitive if you try to touch it.

· Top Tip ·

When my long-haired human has to dry her hair, she uses a magical piece of equipment that blows hot air out of a nozzle. I snuggle into her lap and close my eyes, and all of a sudden I feel like I'm on a beach in the Caribbean and the warm air is tickling my eyebrows. I suggest you try it, it's blissful.

Bearded humans

Some humans may have no hair on the top of their head, but have coarse, bristly beards on their jaws and necks. I have a personal affinity for these humans as I've had a beard since I was a few days old. Grooming-wise, beards are quite high maintenance, as you will need to burrow for any leftover food on a daily basis. Scraps can get lodged in there after every meal, making your human become very smelly.

SCENT

You have to remember that our sense of smell is roughly 1,000 times more powerful than a human's, which may go some way to explaining why we have evolved a more distinguished taste when it comes to all things smelly.

So I'm sure I'm not alone when I admit that I'm partial to a bit of scent. In fact, I never feel like I'm ready to leave the house unless I'm wearing my latest odor.

If I'm flying out the door and don't have the time to splash on anything fancy, I'll take a quick roll through the compost heap in the corner of my garden, as there's usually something extra smelly brewing in there that I know will make me feel fabulous. When I feel like something a bit more special, I've been known to roll in fox poop, and another great tip I learned from my mother was to just stand outside in the rain for five minutes if I've got the time, as the smell of wet dog is like nothing else on this earth.

Stinky spray

Your human, on the other hand, will spray themselves with ghastly manufactured perfumes straight out of the bottle.

This peculiar practice is revolting and you need to try your best to nip it in the bud. As I've addressed already, you need to try and ignore bad behavior and reinforce good, so I suggest you ignore all of these disgusting concoctions (no matter how much they tickle your delicate nostrils) and instead, gently guide your human toward scents and smells that you like.

Scent subterfuge

Fill every corner of your home with the inviting aromas that you favor, and hopefully your taste will begin to rub off on your human. For example, my brother, Rusty, helpfully tucks soggy, sweaty sports socks away underneath the pillows on our guest beds so that they can fill the entire room with their tangy scent. I know that our humans have begun to really appreciate this gesture because when they eventually discover them they let out a howl of pleasure and sometimes even do a joyful little dance.

CHAPTER SEVEN
⊷•⊷

HOW TO DRESS
YOUR HUMAN

HOW TO DRESS YOUR HUMAN

While dogs are fortunate enough to live in a fur coat all day (again, Chinese Crested aside), spare a thought for your human, who is born with no protection against the elements and so must dress themselves every day in especially manufactured clothing. Clothes come in an enormous variety and humans need clothes for every occasion: warm clothes and cozy layers for winter, light fabrics for the heat of summer, sweat-wicking materials for when they exercise, waterproof clothes for going out in the rain, etc., etc.

It's important to allow your human to have freedom of expression when it comes to choosing what clothes to put on at the start of the day, but in the following pages I have outlined a few things to bear in mind. Make sure you encourage your human when they dress in something suitable. Lots of tail-wagging and excitable barking will let them know they've made a good sartorial decision.

Cuddles

Perhaps the most important thing is the fabric. Be wary of dark colors on your human especially if you have a light coat, as molting is never a good look and is a fast track to banishing you from the lap. Velvet and suede make lovely cuddle canvases, but beware of leather as we can scratch it with our claws.

Individuality

It's never a good look to be walking around like twins, so try and guide your human away from clothes that too closely resemble yourself. I've forbidden my humans from wearing tweed, as the brown scratchy fibers are far too similar to my coarse coat. It goes without saying that if you're a Dalmatian, your human should never be seen in polka dots, and so on. The aim is for your human's appearance to complement yours, not compete with it.

BEST CLOTHES

Bare legs

Ankle-exposing skirts and shorts are perfect for leg-licking. Flip-flops and sandals are also wonderful as they allow you to nibble on your human's smelly toes.

Big, warm coats

These should be encouraged because when they've been tossed aside and abandoned on the sofa they make a great place to snuggle up in.

zzZZZZ

Gloves

Not only functional (in keeping your human's hands warm in the cold weather), gloves are also great fun. You can sneak one away when it's been taken off and bury it in the flowerbed for hours of hide-and-seek fun later in the day.

Sneakers and sports shoes

Just wonderful for chewing, the spongy soles of these beauties are perfect for sharpening puppy teeth, and the laces are good fun to unravel.

DOG CLOTHES

Here, I need to draw your attention to a very serious, worrying trend that has been growing in popularity recently. Dog clothing. I'm not sure who is responsible for starting this, but a lot of humans have begun to enjoy putting clothes on us. This behavior seems to manifest itself at novelty times of the year, on holidays such as Christmas, Halloween, and Valentine's Day.

It is fine if you enjoy dressing up, but be aware that behavior can escalate, and while you may have only intended to be wearing a Santa Claus outfit in December, you suddenly find yourself unable to leave the house without being trussed up in a miniature aviator jacket or two pairs of booties. My advice is that you need to have a firm opinion on how you feel about clothing and commit to your decision.

I will not stand for clothes and made it abundantly clear the first time my human tried to put a doggy kimono on me. If, like me, clothes aren't your cup of tea, then my best advice is to stand stockstill, head lowered but eyes glaring up at the ceiling, and simply refuse to move until the offending item has been removed, at which point you should make a show of leaping around like a jolly spring lamb in order to show how relieved you are.

· Important Note ·

This is all personal preference and I wouldn't judge you for a second if you tolerate this behavior—I've seen many a dog happily pounding the pavements in a designer raincoat that matches their human's. Clothes may even bring you closer together, but they aren't something that I am prepared to accept.

CHAPTER EIGHT

MAGGIE'S TEN COMMANDMENTS

And so, dear readers, we're nearing the end of my little guide to how to get the most out of your canine/human relationship. I want to leave you with a few bite-sized nuggets that you can take away for your daily life of human training—I like to view them as my rules to live by, or in other words, my ten commandments:

Never turn down food

As a dog, we aren't always sure where our next meal is coming from. My advice is to eat anything you can get your snout on, and worry about throwing it up on the carpet later. A hungry dog is a grumpy dog, and your relationship with your human (as well as your waistline) will suffer if you decide to pass on that last bit of sausage. Similarly . . .

If it's on the floor, it's edible

This includes chewing gum, leather loafers, cookie crumbs, or human homework. Try it, you might surprise yourself! It's also nice to show your human that you're willing to pull your weight with the housework from time to time, and cleaning up any stray objects you can find is a great way of doing this.

Tennis balls are always for chasing

I'm not suggesting you have to bring them back, but it's your canine obligation to zoom after any fuzzy yellow ball that comes whipping past you. Humans may sometimes try to use tennis balls for their own games, which means you might never get them back, so it's important that you stockpile the ones in your possession in a place that your human can't reach—such as under the sofa or a low-lying coffee table.

When there's a lap available, sit on it

Laps are so much nicer to sit on than cushions (or the floor!), so make your presence felt and climb onto any lap you can find. It's a great (and easy) way of showing your human how much you love them.

And don't worry if you think you're on the large side . . . no dog is ever too big for a cuddle.

Napping is essential

Humans require a patient and tolerant dog to look after them, and so it's essential that you replenish your canine batteries whenever you can so that you are always able to give 100 percent. I like to mix things up, though, and am constantly on the lookout for new and exciting places to catch forty winks. My current favorite spots are the laundry basket and the warm flagstones just in front of the oven in the kitchen.

Constant vigilance

Your home is your castle, so it's important that you're always protecting it. You never know who might swing by, so I suggest you find a good lookout place (I usually choose the back of the sofa in the front room) and devote any free time you have to sentry duty. You should watch out for unpleasant intruders like the mailman or that cat from next door.

Don't watch too much television

Though this can be a lovely opportunity to snuggle up on the sofa and spend some quality time with your human, I know a beagle whose eyes went square from staring at the box too much. Also, watching nature documentaries can raise your heart rate to dangerous levels (I'm always surprised when herds of zebra are suddenly charging across my living room). Drag your human outside instead.

Cats, generally, are the enemy

I approach this with some delicacy as I know there will be some of you who happily share their homes with cats. I'm not claiming that they're all entirely evil, but they are particularly manipulative and shouldn't be totally trusted. Power struggles between the species are not uncommon, and it's important that if you do have to share your home with a feline, you make sure that you are always number one in your human's eyes.

GRRR...

Make yourself heard

Just because humans don't understand our language, it's important that we don't lose our voices. Practice your barking on a daily basis—I like to look at myself in the mirror and yap my head off, practicing for when I have to confront an intruder. Howling along to the radio is also great fun, and your human will really appreciate the sweet sound of your voice.

Make everyone get on your level

Be it human or dog, when I greet people, I like to be nose-to-nose, or nose-to-bottom. I'm a small dog I know, but being on an even standing when communicating is crucial. So I either jump up on my hind legs or expect visitors of the two-legged variety to squat down so we can interact face-to-face.

A FINAL WORD FROM MAGGIE

I may have written a guide for dogs eager to learn how to better develop the bond with their human, but I hope that my readers of the two-legged variety have found my words insightful in some way. Whether you have an actual wet nose or just a metaphorical one, four legs or two, make sure you bound into life's adventures side by side and remember that Man really is a dog's best friend. Especially when Man has a pocket full of treats.

MAGGIE

INDEX

ACKNOWLEDGEMENTS

There are so many people without whom this project would not have been possible. I'd like to thank Louise Lamont for her boundless enthusiasm, Helen Hancocks for not drawing too many cats in this book, Katie Cotton for the help in sounding a lot smarter than I am (grammar is not this dog's strong point) and all of my Border Terrier friends on Twitter for their constant stream of inspiration. I'd also like to thank Kim and Andy for the food and the belly rubs, and my younger brother Rusty for always making me seem like the best behaved dog in our household.